A Guide for Using

The Call of the Wild

in the Classroom

Based on the novel written by Jack London

Written by Philip Denny

Teacher Created Materials, Inc.
6421 Industry Way
Westminster, CA 92683
www.teachercreated.com
©*1995 Teacher Created Materials, Inc.*
Reprinted, 2002
Made in U.S.A.
ISBN-1-55734-446-9

Illustrated by
Agi Palinay

Cover art by
Theresa M. Wright

Edited by
Dona Herweck Rice

Table of Contents

Introduction

A good book can touch our lives like a good friend. Within its pages are words and characters that can inspire us to achieve our highest ideals. We can turn to it for companionship, recreation, comfort, and guidance. It can also give us a cherished story to hold in our hearts forever.

In *Literature Units,* great care has been taken to select books that are sure to become good friends. Teachers who use this unit will find the following features to supplement their own valuable ideas.

- Sample lesson plans

- Pre-reading activities

- A biographical sketch and picture of the author

- A book summary

- Vocabulary lists and suggested vocabulary activities

- Chapters grouped for study with each chapter section including a(n):
    - quiz
    - hands-on project
    - cooperative learning activity
    - cross-curricular connection
    - extension into the reader's own life

- Post-reading activities

- Book report ideas

- Research ideas

- Culminating activity

- Three different options for unit tests

- Bibliography of related reading

- Answer key

We are confident this unit will be a valuable addition to your planning, and we hope your students will increase the circle of "friends" they have in books as you use these ideas.

Sample Lesson Plan

Each of the lessons suggested below can take from one to several days to complete.

Lesson 1

- Introduce and complete some or all of the pre-reading activities found on page 5.
- Read "About the Author" with your students (page 6).
- Read the book summary with your students (page 7).
- Introduce the vocabulary list for Section 1 (page 8) and ask the students to define these words.

Lesson 2

- Read chapter 1. As you read, place the vocabulary words in the context of the story and discuss their meanings.
- Play a vocabulary game (page 9).
- Complete "Concerned Citizens" (page 11).
- Complete "Lost Pet" (page 12).
- Complete "A Study of Contrasts" (page 13).
- Begin "Reading Response Journals" (page14).
- Administer the Section 1 quiz (page 10).
- Introduce the vocabulary list for Section 2 (page 8) and ask the students to define these words.

Lesson 3

- Read chapter 2. Place the vocabulary words in context and discuss their meanings.
- Play a vocabulary game (page 9).
- Complete "Training Time" (page 16).
- Complete "Creating Images" (page 17).
- Complete "Types of Canines" (page 18).
- Complete "The Adaptation" (page 19).
- Administer the Section 2 quiz (page 15).
- Introduce the vocabulary list for Section 3 (page 8) and ask the students to define these words.

Lesson 4

- Read chapters 3 and 4. Place the vocabulary words in context and discuss their meanings.
- Play a vocabulary game (page 9).
- Complete "Diorama of the Sled Team" (page 21).

- Complete "Yukon Territory" (page 22).
- Complete "Explorers and Maps" (page 23).
- Complete "Civilized Behavior" (page 24).
- Administer the Section 3 quiz (page 20).
- Introduce the vocabulary list for Section 4 (page 8) and ask the students to define these words.

Lesson 5

- Read chapter 5. Place the vocabulary words in context and discuss their meanings.
- Play a vocabulary game (page 9).
- Complete "How to Load a Sled" (page 26).
- Complete "Advertising" (page 27).
- Complete "Characterization" (page 28).
- Complete "Pack It Up!" (page 29).
- Administer the Section 4 quiz (page 25).
- Introduce the vocabulary list for Section 5 (page 8) and ask the students to define these words.

Lesson 6

- Read chapters 6 and 7. Place the vocabulary words in context and discuss their meanings.
- Play a vocabulary game (page 9).
- Complete "Camp Menu" (page 31).
- Complete "The Fortune" (page 32).
- Complete "New Ending" (page 33).
- Complete "Bonding" (page 34).
- Administer the Section 5 quiz (page 30).

Lesson 7

- Discuss any questions your students have about the story (page 35).
- Assign book report and research projects (page 36 and 37).
- Begin work on the culminating activities (pages 38, 39, 40, and 41).

Lesson 8

- Discuss the students' enjoyment of the book.
- Administer one, two, or all unit tests (pages 42, 43, and 44).
- Discuss the test answers and possibilities.
- Provide a list of related reading for your students (page 45).

Before the Book

Before you begin reading with your students, do some pre-reading activities to stimulate interest and enhance comprehension. Here are some activities that might work well in your classroom.

1. Predict what the story might be about by hearing the title.

2. Predict what the story might be about by looking at the cover illustration.

3. Discuss other books by Jack London that the students may have heard about or read.

4. Answer these questions:

Are you interested in:

    — *stories about animals?*

    — *stories of loyalty between a dog and its master?*

    — *stories set in the wilds of nature?*

    — *stories of survival?*

    — *stories of action and adventure?*

Would you ever:

    — *be able to navigate a dog sled across Alaska?*

    — *be willing to search for gold alone in the wilderness?*

    — *fish for your dinner?*

    — *be able to build a shelter to last the winter in the snow?*

    — *trust your pet with your life?*

   Work in groups or as a class to create your own story of a dog's loyalty to its master.

About the Author

Jack London was born on January 12, 1876, in San Francisco, California. His father was W.H. Chaney and his mother's name was Flora Wellman. He said that his father was Pennsylvania-born and was alternately a soldier, scout, backwoodsman, trapper, and wanderer. His mother was from Ohio, but his mother and father met and married in San Francisco. Jack eventually took the name of his stepfather.

Jack London's first four years were spent in San Francisco and the next five were spent in the nearby countryside on ranches. He and his family returned to San Francisco when he was nine years old. His parents were poor. From the time he returned to the city on the bay, he had to work. Even when he was only ten years old he had to rise at three o'clock in the morning to get newspapers to sell on the streets before going to school. After school, he did not play or go home. Instead, he went back to get the evening newspaper which he sold sometimes until 10:00 in the evening. Every cent he earned went to his parents.

At 15, Jack left home and school. He later wrote of these early days that he ". . . was a salmon fisher and an oyster pirate." He said that he was a boy in years, but a man among men. By the age of 17, he shipped out on a sealing schooner to hunt for seals off the coasts of Japan and Russia. By the age of 20, the gold fever took him up to the Klondike where he became a prospector for the elusive gold. By the time he was 26, he was a reporter for the Hearst newspaper chain and reported on the Russo-Japanese war. This job did not last long as he went on many sailing adventures to the Caribbean and the South Seas.

From 1907 to 1910, Jack began a round-the-world trip on his new yacht, the *Snark*. He said this was the strongest ship in San Francisco. On the trip, everyone in his crew, including London and his wife, came down with a fever. In fact, the doctors in Australia told him they could do nothing to help them. Their medicines could not combat the various illnesses which they had contracted in the islands they had visited. They returned to the San Francisco Bay area in 1910 where they were able to be in their natural environment and regain their strength.

Jack's literary career developed so fully that his many works and writings are too many to list. Some of his more noteworthy titles include *The Cruise of the Dazzler* (1902), *The Sea Wolf* (1904), *White Fang* (1905), *The Game* (1905), *The Iron Heel* (1907), *The Valley of the Moon* (1913), and *The Meeting of the Elsinore* (1914). He also wrote several short stories of his experiences in the Klondike and his sailing adventures. Many of these short and long works were later turned into movies which can still be seen today. *The Call of the Wild* is among them.

Jack London died in Santa Rosa in 1916.

The Call of the Wild

by Jack London

(Scholastic, 1993)
(Canada and UK; Maxwell Macmillan; AUS, Macmillan)

This is the story of Buck, a one-hundred-forty pound dog who lived in a lordly fashion in the Santa Clara Valley of California. His life changed drastically, completely, and forever when he was kidnapped, thrown on a train, and shipped to Seattle where he was then placed on a ship to Skagway. This was the time of gold fever, and dogs like Buck were in demand as sled dogs up in the Yukon Territory where they were needed to carry men and supplies back and forth from the sea port to the Klondike gold fields.

This story tells of Buck's adaptation to his new, hostile environment and how he reverts to his deep instincts for survival. He learns the way of the new type of men around him. No longer the lord of the manor, he is introduced to the law of the club and whip. These are the tools of the men who own him, and instant obedience prevents these weapons from being turned loose on him.

Along with the new type of owners who claim him in the gold country, there is also a new type of dog. These are not house dogs, but rather they are a throwback to primeval days of old where fighting to the death was the law of survival. Buck learns the new ways and comes to be a sled-team leader as his St. Bernard and shepherd heritage make him a formidable animal. His power comes in his strong mixture of size, speed, and intelligence.

Just before Buck loses touch with civilization and becomes a savage, primitive animal himself, he meets John Thornton who loves him and nurses him back to health. Buck will do anything for John Thornton, and John Thornton is in awe of Buck. Never has John seen such a dog as devoted as Buck. This is proven when "Black" Burton strikes John, only to have Buck leap upon him and tear his throat open. It is proven again when Thornton is swept into the life-killing rapids.

However, as Buck and John go further and further into the wilderness, the call of the wild comes to Buck from the dark forests, from the rivers, and from the earth itself. It is a call that Buck is increasingly drawn to, even if it means leaving his master, John Thornton.

While Buck is gone, yielding to this call, John Thornton and his partners are murdered by Indians. When Buck returns, he wreaks a vengeance on the Yeehats who killed his master. After mourning, he returns to the wild where he becomes leader of a wolf pack. He continues to pursue the Yeehats, and they create a legend about the Ghost Dog who roams at will and kills only Yeehats, and their legend includes the reason why.

Vocabulary Lists

Section 1

arbors	aristocrat	artesian well
conciliate	despatch	dominion
fawn	genial	impartial
imperiously	interlaced	morose
obscurely	perches	pervaded
progeny	resided	resolved
revelation	trice	uncouth
unkempt	veranda	wan

Section 2

antagonist	appeasement	arduous
belligerent	blunder	cadence
consternation	courier	diabolical
dignity	disconsolate	draught
forlorn	imperative	indiscretion
indispensable	intentness	instincts
malignant	primeval	primordial
scarlet	surged	vicarious

Section 3

abjectly	brute	compel
contemplation	convulsive	daunted
exultant	fang	slavered
grievously	jugular	malinger
mates	nocturnal	pandemonium
perplexed	poise	potent
precipitate	rashness	resiliency
	shirked	

Section 4

apprehensive	cajole	callowness
cell	cherish	chronic
clannish	commence	dismay
dwindle	fatigue	feigned
implore	indeterminate	interval
jaded	mongrel	recital
shorn	slovenly	superfluous
thoroughfare	unwieldy	

Section 5

abundance	communion	contagion
convalescence	demonstrative	entice
equilibrium	expediency	exploit
keenest	impede	indiscreet
lope	mandate	manifested
melancholy	ministrations	miscalculate
pertinacity	plethoric	pompous
quest	romp	stately
vigil	wiliness	

8

Vocabulary Activity Ideas

You can help your students learn and retain the vocabulary in *The Call of the Wild* by providing them with interesting vocabulary activities. Here are a few ideas to try.

❑ People of all ages like to make and solve puzzles. Ask your students to make their own **crossword puzzles** or **word search puzzles,** using the vocabulary words from the story.

❑ Challenge your students to a **vocabulary bee**. This is similar to a spelling bee, but in addition to spelling each word correctly, the game participants must correctly define the words as well.

❑ Play **vocabulary concentration**. The goal of this game is to match vocabulary words with their definitions. Divide the class into groups of 2–5 students. Have the students make two sets of cards the same size and color. On one set, have them write the vocabulary words. On the second set, have them write the definitions. All cards are mixed together and placed face down on a table. A player picks two cards. If the pair matches the word with its definition, the player keeps the cards and takes another turn. If the pair does not match, the player turns the cards face down once more, and the next player takes his or her turn. Players must concentrate to remember the locations of the words and their definitions. The game continues until all matches have been made. This is an ideal activity for free exploration time.

❑ Have your students practice their writing skills by creating sentences and paragraphs in which multiple vocabulary words are used correctly. Ask them to share their compact **vocabulary sentences** and paragraphs with the class.

❑ Ask your students to create paragraphs which use the vocabulary words to present **history lessons** that relate to the time period or historical events mentioned in the story.

❑ Challenge your students to **use a specific vocabulary word** from the story at least 10 times in one day. They must keep a record of when and how the word was used.

❑ As a group activity, have the students work together to create an **illustrated dictionary** of the vocabulary words.

❑ Play **20 Clues** with the entire class. In this game, one student selects a vocabulary word and gives clues about this word, one by one, until someone in the class can guess the word.

❑ Play **vocabulary charades.** In this game, vocabulary words are pantomimed.

You probably have many more ideas to add to this list. Try them! See if experiencing vocabulary on a personal level increases your students' vocabulary interest and retention.

Quiz

1. On the back of this paper, write a one-paragraph summary of the major events in this chapter.

2. What is Buck's life like at the judge's home?

    _____

    _____

3. What breed of dog is Buck?

    _____

4. What did Manuel do that got him into debt?

    _____

    _____

5. Why does Buck go willingly with Manuel?

    _____

    _____

6. Why does the stranger lie to the baggageman on the train and say that the dog has fits?

    _____

    _____

7. Where does the train take Buck?

    _____

8. How does the man in the red sweater train Buck?

    _____

    _____

9. What does Buck learn from the man?

    _____

    _____

10. How does Buck react to the snow when he is taken to Alaska?

    _____

    _____

Concerned Citizens

Buck had an ideal life in the Santa Clara Valley on Judge Miller's grounds. In fact, the author informs us that Buck lived the life of an "aristocrat" and was a "king" of sorts over the other animals that lived on the judge's estate with him. The dignity which Buck was afforded during those four years of his life was quickly stripped away from him when he was kidnapped by Manuel and sold to the stranger at the little train station at College Park.

1. Brainstorm as a class and list on the chalkboard the various acts of cruelty that Buck endured at the hands of the stranger, while in the care of the saloonkeeper, and on his trip to Seattle. Next, brainstorm and list the cruel "training" that he received at Seattle from the next tormentor, the stout man with the red sweater.

2. Working in appropriately-sized cooperative learning groups, pick one of the most disturbingly cruel things done to Buck and make a poster protesting this type of behavior. This poster can be painted on a 2' x 3' (60 cm x 90 cm) piece of butcher paper. Make sure the picture captures the cruel situation that Buck is enduring and that it has a fitting message placed to help make your point.

3. Brainstorm as a class again to discover other types of animal cruelty about which people are concerned about. This list can be placed on the chalkboard to refer to for the next activity.

4. With your cooperative learning group, pick three of the other types of animal cruelty from the chalkboard. On the space provided below, label each type of animal cruelty and provide an appropriate punishment for the offender or offenders.

Cruelty	Punishment

Lost Pet

Buck was a great favorite at the Miller household. His loss must have had an effect on everyone.

1. For this activity, you will be working in a cooperative learning group. Together, write how the disappearance of Buck affected each of the following members of the household. (To better understand the characters and their feelings, reread the pages near the beginning of chapter one that show how these people interrelated with Buck.)

Judge Miller: _____

Judge Miller's boys: _____

Mollie and Alice: _____

2. For this next activity, work together and pretend that you are the judge. Recall all the characteristics and qualities of Buck. In the space provided, write a "Lost Dog" advertisement for the local newspaper. Be specific. You will need to come up with an estimated date and time of the disappearance as well as the dog's name and any reward that you think would be appropriate.

Lost Dog

A Study of Contrasts

Part of the literary artist's skill in showing the great injustices done to Buck is accomplished by contrasting just how wonderful his life was before the kidnapping with what happened after it. In this case, Jack London wrote four pages depicting the dog's heritage, his regal surroundings, and even the financial situation of his owners. All these paint the picture of an untroubled, carefree life for Buck. Then, Jack London writes of the murky character, Manuel, and of his connection to gambling and the underworld characters associated with the theft of the trusting Buck. With sudden abruptness, Buck is choked, caged, tormented, and starved, only to be released and beaten again unmercifully by the man in the red sweater. Truly, Buck's world up to this point is one of great contrasts.

Let us imagine that the editors of the book wanted to underscore this contrast even further. They determined that if the book's cover had an illustration of the two worlds with which Buck would be confronted, the book would appeal to the prospective buyer's sense of curiosity. This would result in more sales and a higher profit margin for their company.

For this activity you and your partner are to draw a picture that reflects the author's written picture of Buck's life on the judge's estate in the Santa Clara Valley. Your picture should include one or more of the activities that were pleasant ones for Buck and the Millers. Next to that picture, find any of the scenes in which Buck is no longer the king of his realm. This picture should be one where Buck is the victim of one of his tormentors as related by the author. Both pictures should be true to form as related by the words of Jack London in the first chapter.

Share your work with the class. You might also display it in your classroom or school library.

Reading Response Journals

One effective way to ensure that the reading of *The Call of the Wild* touches each student in a personal way is to include the use of Reading Response Journals in your plans. In these journals, students can be encouraged to respond to the story in a number of ways.

First, ask the students to create a journal for *The Call of the Wild*. Initially, have them assemble lined and unlined, three-holed paper in a brad-fastened report cover with a blank page for the journal's cover. As they read the story, they may draw designs on the cover that help tell the story for them. Tell the students that the purpose of the journal is to record their thoughts, ideas, observations, and questions as they read. Provide students with, or ask them to suggest, topics from the story that stimulate writing. Here are two examples from the Section 1 chapter:

> *When Buck first encountered snow, he did not know what it was. "It bit like fire." The onlookers laughed. Can you remember a time when you were embarrassed as you tried something for the first time? What was it like?*

> *Buck trusted everyone in the beginning of the story. He even trusted the man who sold him. Do you trust everyone you know? How do you know when it is safe to trust someone?*

Here are a few suggestions for using the journals:

- After reading each chapter, the students can write one or more new things they learned from the chapter.
- The students can draw their responses to certain events or characters in the story by using the blank pages in their journals.
- Tell the students that they may use their journals to record diary-type responses. Encourage them to bring their journal ideas to life. Ideas generated from their journal writing can be used to create plays, debates, stories, songs, and art displays.
- Allow students time to write in their journals daily.

Explain to the students that their Reading Response Journals can be evaluated in a number of ways. Here are a few ideas:

1. Personal reflections will be read by the teacher, but no corrections or letter grades will be assigned. Credit is given for effort, and all students who sincerely try will be awarded credit. If a grade is desired for this type of entry, you can grade according to the number of journal entries compared to the number of journal assignments. For example, if five journal assignments were made and the student conscientiously completes all five, then he or she can receive an "A."
2. Non-judgmental teacher responses should be made as you read the journals to let the students know that you are reading and enjoying their journals. Here are some types of responses that will please your journal writers and encourage them to write more.
   — "You have really found what's important in the story."
   — "You write so clearly I almost feel as if I am there."
   — "You seem to be able to learn from this book and apply what you learn to your life."

3. If you would like to grade something for form and content, ask the students to select one of their entries and polish it according to the writing process.

Quiz

1. On the back of this paper, write a one-paragraph summary of the major events of this section.

2. What happened to Curly that later gave Buck nightmares?

   _____

   _____

3. What did Buck learn from Curly's tragedy?

   _____

   _____

4. Why couldn't Buck find the other dogs from his team that first night in the snow?

   _____

   _____

5. Why did Perrault particularly need the best sled dogs for his job?

   _____

   _____

6. What purpose did Francois have in putting Buck between the other sled dogs, Dave and Sol-leks?

   _____

   _____

7. When the author wrote that "Francois' whip snapped less frequently," what was the meaning of that statement?

   _____

   _____

8. Why did Buck quickly forget his fastidiousness in his eating habits and eat his food as quickly as possible?

   _____

   _____

9. Why did Buck begin to hate Spitz?

   _____

   _____

10. What trick did Buck learn from Pike which he would never have done at the judge's household?

    _____

    _____

Training Time

(**Teacher note:** Because this activity requires the actual training of dogs, you may wish to offer it as an extra credit assignment.)

While much has been written about Buck being royally treated in Santa Clara, little is mentioned about his training. After he is kidnapped, we see that he learns what a club and an ax can do to shape his behavior. Later, he learns to obey largely due to the sting of Francois' whip. Finally, he learns by the biting and mauling of the other dogs, Dave and Sol-leks. He is an apt learner. In Chapter 2, Francois even offers, "Dat Buck for sure learn queek as anything."

There are many ways to train a dog, as evidenced above. Yet, to reach a quality relationship between dog and master, the training must be built on rewards. Every dog wants to do the right things to please its masters. To reach this end, it needs to be trained in the types of behavior that are appropriate to living with humans. This type of training requires rewards (praise or treats) and great patience. By providing this on a consistent basis, your dog will become a well-behaved friend and a valued "member" of your family.

For this activity, you will need a dog. As you have read, this dog does not need to be a puppy to be trained, although the younger the better. If you have your own dog to train, so much the better, but if not, you might borrow the dog of a neighbor or friend.

You will need to find a place in the park that is quiet with little or no distractions. Your own backyard will work if a park is unavailable. You will need only about 10 minutes for each training session, as the dog can concentrate only for about that long. You should try to do your training about the same time each day.

The "Stay" and "Come" Commands

Go to your dog's training spot with your dog's leash in place. Once there, stop. Then, gently push your dog's rear down into the sitting position and say, "Stay." If he attempts to get up, get his attention again and repeat the gesture, placing your pet back into the sitting position and saying, "Stay."

If your dog tries to lie down, repeat the gesture but hold up the leash. This will place him in the sitting position. Once you have him in this position, pet him and repeat the command. Next, lay down the leash and repeat the command. Then, walk a few feet away, keeping eye contact and repeating the command. Then, call the dog by its name and give the command, "Come!" When the dog comes, place it in the sitting position and reward with praise. Pet your dog enthusiastically.

You should repeat the steps outlined above several times each session. As your dog begins to understand what it is to do, you will be able to command it to stay for increasingly longer distances and time.

Remember, all dogs want to please their masters. If your dog becomes confused or excessively restless, break off the session for the day. Also note that even though your dog will respond well to doggie treats, praise and physical affection will be just as rewarding to your pet.

Creating Images

Imagery is a form of figurative language that creates mental images. Jack London uses extensive imagery to help make the story more real for the reader so that the reader can see what Buck is seeing. An example of his use of imagery is evidenced early in Chapter 2:

> " . . . *Buck was taken aback. He saw Spitz run out his scarlet tongue in a way he had of laughing; and he saw Francois, swinging an axe, spring into the mess of dogs. Three men with clubs were helping to scatter them. It did not take long. Two minutes from the time Curly went down, the last of her assailants were clubbed off. But she lay there limp and lifeless in the bloody, trampled snow, almost literally torn to pieces, the swart half-breed standing over her and cursing horribly.*"

This scene is so vividly described that it is as though the reader is actually living it.

Now, it is your turn. Working with a partner, you are to locate three similar examples of imagery from Chapter 2. You and your partner will find the examples and write them down entirely. Then, on a separate sheet of paper, draw a visual representation of one of your examples.

Example 1: _____

_____

_____

_____

_____

_____

Example 2: _____

_____

_____

_____

_____

_____

Example 3: _____

_____

_____

_____

_____

_____

Types of Canines

By now, you are aware that there are many types of canines. Several of the larger breeds are chosen for the difficult work of being sled dogs. Others are mixed breeds, like Buck. Buck's mother was a Scotch Shepherd and his father was a St. Bernard.

Brainstorm as a class the different types of canines that you know. Working in cooperative learning groups, classify them according to their originating countries. Also, provide a brief description of each. You may need to consult the encyclopedia for this organizational activity.

Type of Dog	Brief Description	Place of Origin

Teacher note: After the students have completed their charts, you may wish to assign each individual or pair a canine to research in depth. The students can then make reports to the class.

The Adaptation

It is said that our environment shapes all of us. This certainly seems to be true of Buck. The author tells us that Buck had " . . . been suddenly jerked from the heart of civilization and flung into the heart of things primordial." He goes on to remind the reader that now Buck had to be constantly alert, " . . . for these dogs and men were not town dogs and men. They were savages, all of them, who knew no law but the law of club and fang."

Answer the following questions:

1. Just what does the author mean when he says, ". . . these dogs and men were not town dogs and men"?

   _____

   _____

2. What examples does the author give to back up his statement that ". . . they were savages, all of them, who knew no law but the law of club and fang"?

   _____

   _____

3. Now that Buck is in this environment, do you think he becomes one of the "savages"? Be prepared to explain your answer with evidence to the class.

   _____

   _____

4. Discuss whether or not you think Buck had any choice in the changes from his earlier behavior. As time progressed, Buck would steal and let another take the blame. His moral decay continued as he abandoned such civilized attributes as love and fellowship. He also took no more notice of personal feelings or private property. Had he not made these adaptations to his life, do you think he would have survived?

   _____

   _____

Consider the following questions for class discussion:

1. How have you been shaped by your environment?
2. Have you ever been shaped by a hostile, unfriendly environment? What did you do? Did you have to change to the way the majority acted? Why?
3. Have you ever been shaped by the influence of a nice, friendly environment? What were the circumstances?
4. How can peer pressure influence you positively? Negatively?
5. How can your early family teachings on moral convictions help you through rough times?

Quiz

1. On the back of this paper, write a paragraph summarizing the major events in each chapter of this section (two paragraphs in all).

2. Why did Spitz go out of its way to snarl at and bully Buck?

    _____

    _____

3. What actually happened that started the first fight between Buck and Spitz?

    _____

    _____

4. What took place in the middle of the fight that stopped it?

    _____

    _____

5. Why was the Thirty Mile River considered to be the hardest part of the trail?

    _____

    _____

6. Why did the technique Perrault devised, though effective, cost them so much valuable time?

    _____

    _____

7. What did the dog-driver do for Buck to help solve the problem of Buck's sore feet?

    _____

    _____

8. Before Dolly chased Buck, how did she let it be known that she had gone mad?

    _____

    _____

9. How did the breaking down of the dogs' discipline affect the dog team?

    _____

    _____

10. What did Buck do to Spitz that meant certain death for his old foe?

    _____

    _____

Diorama of the Sled Team

These two chapters have many exciting and memorable scenes in them. There are the fights between Spitz and Buck, the journey over Thirty Mile River, Perrault plunging through the ice, and the attack by the huskies on the sled team and others.

As a class, brainstorm all of the exciting moments of the last two chapters. Then, for the next activity, break into cooperative learning groups to prepare a diorama of the most exciting event, as decided upon by you and your group. Follow the steps below.

1. Decide together what scene you would like to dramatize and sketch it out on a piece of paper.

2. Obtain a shoebox or another box of similar size.

3. Measure the dimensions of the bottom of the box and cut out a piece of white butcher paper to that exact size.

4. Now, draw your final drawing of your diorama background on that same paper and glue it to the bottom of your diorama box.

5. Turn your box on its side. You now have the completed background that you need before inserting the additions to your diorama.

6. Using as many natural materials as possible, begin constructing your scene. Be creative with your work. A piece of aluminum might represent a section of the river. Cotton might represent the snow. Plexiglass can become the ice, and you can use toothpicks to construct the sled itself.

7. After the diorama is complete, present it to the class.

Extension

Along with your diorama, you are to provide a tape recording of what is taking place. You and your partners are to devise an exciting interpretation of what is happening. Make it fun and dramatic, using all members of your group. You can imitate the growling and snapping of the dogs, or you might be Perrault yelling for help or Francois commanding the dogs to mush.

Yukon Territory

The Yukon Territory was harsh and unforgiving. In the novel, it wears down Dave, particularly because the sled drivers are relentless in moving their supplies. They do so at the expense of their dogs, which seem to be expendable to them.

The Yukon Territory with which Buck is acquainted is the area from the sea town of Skagway up and over White Pass and on to Dawson, which was where the Klondike strike took place. This great gold find brought over 30,000 adventurers looking for the precious mineral, and it did so in just two years. A closer look at this vast area will help to gain greater understanding as to the ordeal the dogs and men undergo in the novel.

For this activity, you and a partner will need a geography book or an encyclopedia to find the appropriate answers for the blanks below. Careful attention to chapters 3 and 4 of *The Call of the Wild* may also prove helpful to you.

The Yukon Territory is triangular in shape. The territory immediately to its east is called the _____ Territory. To the south is the province called _____ Columbia. To the west is the state called _____.
The sea up north is the _____. This territory received its name because the _____ River flows across it.

The geology of the territory is primarily that of a high _____.
Except for the west, this is made of the Ogilvie Mountains and in the south there is the _____ Range. This range includes Mount _____, which rises to the dizzying height of 19,850 feet (5,955 m) above sea level and is the highest peak in _____. To the east are the two ranges named the _____ Mountains and the _____ Mountains.

Gold was discovered in 1881 at the Big _____ River. The big strike on the _____ Plateau began in 1886. People rushed to the territory. Due to the harsh conditions, traveling was difficult and the need for sled dogs was paramount. _____, a site near the gold strike, was named the capital of the Yukon Territory in 1898. As the importance of this area lessened, the seat of government changed to the present day capitol of _____, which it has been since the year 1953.

Word Bank

Alaska	Yukon	plateau	Saint Elias
Northwest	Salmon	Whitehorse	Klondike
Dawson	British	Beaufort Sea	Logan
	Canada	Mackenzie	Selwyn

Explorers and Maps

Early pathfinders were instrumental in the settlement of the area described in *The Call of the Wild*. One who was very influential was Captain Vancouver. He navigated the Pacific Northwest in the 1700s and made it possible for new settlers to arrive by ship and head toward the Yukon to seek their fortunes. Another influential pathfinder was Sir Alexander Mackenzie, a partner in a fur company as well as an ardent explorer. The Mackenzie River was named after him because he had traced it to the Arctic Ocean by canoe. The Mackenzie Mountain Range and the Mackenzie Bay at the inlet of his river were also named after this explorer and adventurer.

What these and other explorers have in common is that they made it possible for others to follow in their direction. By exploring the land, each made it easier for those who came next to settle the area. To settle the area effectively, however, the course needed to be accurately charted. The maps created by the explorers were all that others had to follow to reach their destinations.

Below are the areas the author writes about that are located between the main points of Skagway and Dawson. They are not given in the correct order, however. Your task is to put them in their correct geographic sequence just as Buck and his sled team would have encountered them on their trip. Create a map in the frame below, showing the locations of each of these spots.

• Little Salmon	• Lake Tagish	• Pelly Rink Rapids	• White Pass
• Lake LeBarge	• Five Fingers	• Lake Bennett	• White Horse Rapids
• Thirty Mile River	• Sixty Miles	• Skagway	• Lake Marsh

Civilized Behavior

From the time Buck leaves the serenity of the Santa Clara Valley, he must compromise his civility. He no longer eats with the decorum of the princely dog that he is. He becomes a thief and, worse yet, a "primordial beast" who has made his kill and "found it good." When Buck fights, he now knows that he should fight to the death to keep his adversary out of the way. The author is attempting to show what can happen to even a well-behaved animal if the conditions are bad enough.

This disintegration of civilized behavior is evident in human beings, as well. Whenever there is excess stress in living conditions, overcrowding, or a sense of helplessness, people act out their own savage instincts, too. Rarely is this done in the extreme as it is between Buck and Spitz, but there are often angry words that erupt, just like the snarls exchanged by the dogs. There are also fights that take place if reason and humanity do not intervene.

How does civilized behavior disintegrate in everyday life? As a class, brainstorm to determine common sources of friction among brothers and sisters. Afterwards, in the space provided below, pick three of the most common sources of friction and next to each provide some methods (perhaps those used by your own family) to solve the problems.

Problem	Solution
1.	
2.	
3.	

Extension: What are some common sources of irritation here at school that can erupt in fights among students?

Quiz

1. On the back of this paper, write a paragraph summarizing the major events in this chapter.

2. Why does the journey take twice as long on this trip from Dawson to Skagway?

    _____

    _____

3. Describe the condition of the dogs as they enter Skagway.

    _____

    _____

4. How many days of rest do the dogs get in their last 1,800 miles?

    _____

    _____

5. What does Buck's first impression of his new owner's camp tell about the new owners?

    _____

    _____

6. The dogs need about two weeks rest before another run to Dawson, but how much time do they actually get?

    _____

    _____

7. How do the new owners pack the sled, and what is the result?

    _____

    _____

8. What advice do the seasoned citizens of Skagway give the new sled owners?

    _____

    _____

9. What kind of outlook does the team have when the new dogs arrive, and why is that?

    _____

    _____

10. At the end of Chapter 5, the statement is made, "The bottom had dropped out of the trail." What does this mean?

    _____

    _____

How to Load a Sled

Hal and Charles are inexperienced sled men, and the mountainous load that they pile on their sled reflects this fact. They do not lash down the load tightly, so when they hit the first turn the sled flips onto its side, spilling the goods as the dogs run on down the main street of Skagway. They also mistreat the dogs by whipping them because they think the dogs are being lazy. The fact is, however, that they are just too inexperienced to know they must break the sled's runners out of the frozen snow.

As a class, discuss what other things Jack London wrote about that let you know these people do not belong on the tough trail to Dawson. Also discuss the types of items that Hal and Charles end up taking out of their sled. Why do they feel that they do not need these items?

Now, with a partner, pretend that you are two of Skagway's officials. It is your job to prepare a poster showing the proper items to be put on a sled for a Dawson run. Not only are you to include the mail but also the things necessary for survival and their placement on the sled. Use the space below to list all the items that are needed for a Dawson run. Include the amount of food that should be provided for each dog on a daily basis. Also include the amount of food needed by each individual for a twenty-day trip. What will individuals carry, and what can they find while on their trip?

On a separate piece of paper, make an illustration of the sled with a diagram showing where the items are to be stored. It is only after these qualifications have been met that a dog sled team will be allowed out of Skagway.

Necessities

Advertising

For this activity, you and your cooperative learning group are to pretend that you have been contracted to advertise an exciting new book, *The Call of the Wild.* What your employers want is a series of sketches that might catch the flavor of the book as well as the interest of the perspective readers.

Brainstorm with your partners to come up with some ideas that will show the action of the story. Try to think of creative graphics that will dramatically show the title and author of the book as well. Show some of your ideas in the box.

Next, on separate paper, sketch three of your advertising ideas. Remember, this is not a book cover. These are ideas for an advertisement that might be in a magazine or on a poster at a bookstore. All that is wanted are illustrations of the type of art and graphics that you have in mind for an advertisement.

After you have completed your sketches, decide as a group which sketch is the best. Now, create the advertisement in its final form on a piece of butcher paper or poster board. Choose colors that will add interest to the ad.

Characterization

Characterization is an author's way of depicting the actors in a story. It is a technique an author uses to add color or depth to his characters. Working like an artist at a canvas, the author first sketches his character lightly. This allows the reader to become involved and to visualize the character. As the story unfolds, the author adds a stroke of color here and a highlight there, making the depth of the character come into a sharper focus. By the time the author has completed his "drawing," the reader knows all the qualities and weaknesses of the character.

The following is an example of characterization from earlier in the story:

> *"Manuel, one of the gardener's helpers, was an undesirable acquaintance. Manuel had one besetting sin. He loved to play Chinese lottery. Also, in his gambling, he had one besetting weakness—faith in a system; and this made his damnation certain."*

Characterization: Manuel is undesirable, a gambler, and none too bright. He is also doomed.

Now it is your turn. For the characters listed below, find similar examples of characterization in Chapter 5 of the book. Copy each quote and then tell what characteristic is being demonstrated in it.

Character	Quote	Characteristics
Hal		
Mercedes		
John Thornton		

After you have completed the chart, share your ideas with the class and see whether others agree with your analysis of the three characters.

Pack It Up!

Buck thought he did not have the best of it when Francois and Perrault sold his services to the Scotch half-breed, but when he is sold to the likes of Hal and Charles, he knows true misery.

They are uneducated in the ways of the Yukon, and the dogs bear the brunt of their ignorance and cruelty. One of the first evidences of how long and difficult the next trip will be is the manner in which the sled is loaded. It is loaded in a helter-skelter manner with no thought as to how it will ride. It has too much gear in it, and it holds many things that are useless to the travelers on the trail. Moreover, it is unbalanced with heavy, bulky items packed on top. Some of the necessary items are buried on the bottom, and the whole sled must be unpacked just to reach what is necessary.

Packing, whether it be for a day hike in the mountains or for a day at the beach, requires a little thought. You need to prepare a list of things you will need and then place them in the backpack with the heavy items on the bottom.

As a class, brainstorm the types of things that you might take with you for a day hike on a mountain trail. Consider the weight and keep in mind the necessary safety items as well as the other obvious things.

One-day outings are relatively easy to prepare for. But a three-day trip to the mountains would be different. You would need sleeping gear as well as some type of cooking utensils and food. Working alone or in pairs, make a list of everything you would need for a three-night backpacking trip to the mountains. Remember that you are not going to a luxury hotel, and you must take everything that is necessary to be comfortable in a mountain environment.

Quiz

1. On the back of this paper, write a paragraph summarizing the major events in each of these chapters (two paragraphs in all).

2. Why does Buck love John Thornton more than any of his masters?

    _____

    _____

3. What is the lesson that Buck teaches "Black" Burton?

    _____

    _____

4. Describe how Buck receives three cracked ribs while saving John Thornton's life.

    _____

    _____

5. Why do the men from the Eldorado Saloon throw their hats and mittens in the air and bubble over in "incoherent babel"?

    _____

    _____

6. What prompts John Thornton and his partners to travel east and leave Dawson?

    _____

    _____

7. What would it have meant if the men found the old Lost Cabin?

    _____

    _____

8. What happens back at the camp while Buck is returning from hunting his moose?

    _____

    _____

9. Why does Buck have such a sense of pride after what he does to the Yeehats?

    _____

    _____

10. Why do the Yeehats refer to Buck as the Evil Spirit?

    _____

    _____

Camp Menu

While looking for the Lost Cabin, John Thornton and his partners travel and hunt in Indian fashion. This means that they hunt for their dinner in the course of a day's travel. If they fail to find any food, they go without. They are secure in the knowledge that eventually they will come upon game.

Today, there are seasons for hunting, and it is only permissible in certain areas. When we go camping, we take along a Dutch oven or there is a fire pit complete with a grill to cook our food. Some campers even have a lightweight camping stove which takes a bottle of propane to ignite.

Discuss some of the ways to cook or prepare food while camping. If you have never been camping, then discuss what you have heard about camping. What are some tried and true breakfasts that you know are great in the woods? What foods will help to give you a good night's sleep?

Now, join with a partner. You two are going to create a recipe for a breakfast and a dinner at the camping location of your choice. Describe the setting (mountain, desert, etc.) where you and your partner will be camping and what will be your principal way of cooking (no travel trailers or electricity allowed). Also, describe the camp site and tell where it is located. For example, are you in the High Sierra or in the Sawtooth Mountains of Idaho? Be specific.

Next, give the names of the meals and describe the recipes that you will use to complete this camping experience.

Location:

Recipes:

The Fortune

In chapters 6 and 7, you read of loyalty, courage, and luck. John Thornton finds the gold he is looking for, and he and his friends put thousands of dollars worth of gold dust into moosehide bags every day. Each bag weighs fifty pounds, and these are piled up outside their spruce-bough lodge like firewood.

Assuming that these adventurers were like normal men, there probably came a time when they discussed just how much money they had in their "stack of firewood." Since the author did not put a figure on it, you can do it yourself. But first, you will need to learn a thing or two about troy weight.

Troy weight is the standard measurement for gold. In it, a pound is made of 12 ounces, and a pound is equal to .3732 kilograms. The ounce is equal to 20 pennyweight. The pennyweight equals 24 grains. Using the above information, answer the following questions.

1. How much is one pound of gold dust worth if an ounce is worth $100.00?

   _____

2. If a moosehide bag holds 50 pounds, how much is one bag of gold worth?

   _____

3. If the adventurers had 50 full bags next to their shelter, how much money would that represent?

   _____

4. What if they had 75 bags filled with the gold?

   _____

5. How much would each man receive if they cashed in the 75 bags of gold down in Dawson, assuming that the price is still $100.00 per ounce?

   _____

6. If the price went up to $150.00 per ounce, what would be the total value of one pound?

   _____

7. How much would one bag be worth?

   _____

8. How much would 50 bags be worth?

   _____

9. How much would the 75 bags be worth?

   _____

10. What would each man's share be for the 75 bags?

   _____

New Ending

Thornton and his friends do not get to take their gold to town. They are murdered before this grand day comes about.

For the next assignment, pretend that the publisher of *The Call of the Wild* does not care for the ending of the story, believing that it leaves the reader with too negative a feeling. Working in small cooperative groups, it is your task to rewrite the ending of the story. You are to begin your new ending with Buck returning to the camp. He still smells that something is going on, but it is not the death of his master, Thornton.

In the space provided below, write the new ending of the story, and to satisfy your publisher, it must be an ending that will be pleasing to the reader and not depressing. Use additional paper, if necessary.

Bonding

The love between Buck and his master, John Thornton, is very great. Buck will do whatever John asks of him, even to jumping off a cliff when commanded to do so. He almost kills himself when rescuing Thornton from certain death in the rapids. When the call of the forest pulls him away for longer and longer periods of time, Buck always rouses himself and runs back to Thornton's camp.

As a class, discuss how Thornton must feel when his dog leaves for ever-increasing periods of time. Do you think that his companions ever mention it to Thornton? Do they realize that the call of the wild is getting stronger than the bond between Thornton and his dog?

In the space provided below, write an attempt by Thornton's friends to show him why he should give up the dog and let it follow its instincts, to return to the call. Include Thornton's reaction to their plea.

After you have written the dialogue, explain your reasoning for Thornton's response.

Any Questions?

When you finished reading *The Call of the Wild*, did you have some questions that were left unanswered? Write some of those questions here.

_____

_____

_____

_____

_____

Work in groups or by yourself to prepare possible answers for some or all of the questions you have asked above as well as those written below. When you have finished your paper, share your ideas with the class.

1. Does Manuel ever get caught for stealing the judge's dog?

2. Does Manuel's wife know how evil he is?

3. What does the judge do when he finds out his dog is gone?

4. Does he have any suspicions as to who might have stolen Buck?

5. Does the judge get a new dog right away?

6. Were the remains of Thornton's group ever found?

7. Will Buck keep killing the Yeehats?

8. Does he kill only those who were responsible for the murder of his master?

9. Do the prospectors in Dawson ever wonder about Thornton's disappearance?

10. Is a search party ever sent to look for Thornton and his friends?

11. How long would it take for the bags of gold to dissolve back into the earth?

12. Does Buck ever again find human companionship?

13. Does Buck become a wolf?

14. Does Buck ever think of the judge or John Thornton again?

15. Is Buck happier in the wilds than he is with Thornton?

16. Will someone else find the little valley with the gold in it?

17. Would Thornton's group have been able to get their gold to Dawson?

18. Would there be a chance of being robbed if they returned to their strike for more gold?

19. Did Thornton like looking for gold more than finding it?

20. Did they look for gold as a pasttime and really just prefer being in each other's company out in the wilderness?

21. What would a man like Thornton do with all that money?

22. Will Buck return to civilization before he dies?

23. Will Buck teach his offspring to kill the Indians, too?

24. Has Buck become a wild dog forever?

Book Report Ideas

There are numerous ways to do a book report. After you have finished reading *The Call of the Wild*, choose one method of reporting that interests you. It may be a way that your teacher suggests, an idea of your own or one of the ways mentioned below.

See What I Read?

This report is a visual one. A model of a scene from the story can be created, or a likeness of one or more of the characters from the story can be drawn or sculpted.

Time Capsule

This report provides people living at a future time with the reason *The Call of the Wild* is such an outstanding book, and it gives these future people reasons why it should be read. Make a time capsule design and neatly print or write your reasons inside the capsule. You may wish to bury your capsule after you have shared it with your classmates. Perhaps one day someone will find it and read *The Call of the Wild* because of what you wrote!

Come to Life!

This report is one that lends itself to a group project. The group acts out a scene from the story and relates the significance of the scene to the entire book. Costumes and props will add to the dramatization.

A Letter to the Publisher

In this report, you can write a letter to Jack London's publisher. Tell the publisher what you liked about *The Call of the Wild* and ask them any questions you may have about the writing of the book. You might want to give the publisher some suggestions for a sequel. After your teacher has read it, and you have made your writing the best it can be, send it to the publisher.

Guess Who or What

This report takes the form of several games of 20 Questions. The reporter gives a series of general to specific clues about a character from the story, and the students guess the identity of the mystery character. After the character has been identified, the same reporter presents another 20 questions about an event in the story.

A Character Comes to Life

Suppose one of the characters in *The Call of the Wild* came to life and walked into your home or classroom. This report describes what this character sees, hears, and feels as he or she experiences the world in which you live.

Coming Attraction

The Call of the Wild is about to be made into a movie, and you have been chosen to design the promotional poster. Include the title and the author of the book, a listing of the main characters, the contemporary actors who will play the characters, a drawing of a scene from the book, and a paragraph synopsis of the story.

Literary Interview

This report is done in pairs. One student pretends to be a character in the story. The other student will play the role of a television or radio interviewer, providing the audience with insights into the character's personality and life. It is the responsibility of the partners to create meaningful questions and appropriate responses.

Research

As you are reading *The Call of the Wild,* you will encounter geographical locations, dog-training techniques, culturally and philosophically diverse people, and a variety of animals. To increase your understanding of the characters and events in the story as well as more fully recognizing Jack London's craft as a writer, research to find out more about these people, places, and things. Work in groups to research fully one of the areas mentioned below or your own idea. Share your findings with the rest of the class in any appropriate manner of oral presentation.

- Yukon Territory
- Yukon Trail
- Yukon River
- Tahkeena River
- Mackenzie Mountains
- Mackenzie River
- Mackenzie Bay
- Northwest Territory
- Northwest Mounted Police
- gold
- Klondike gold fields
- mining towns
- aurora borealis
- Alaska
- Skagway
- Dawson
- White Pass
- tundra
- Arctic Ocean
- Alexander Mackenzie
- Captain Vancouver
- Sled dogs
- Types of sleds
- Habits and environment of . . .

moose	white-tailed deer	caribou
elk	otter	grizzly bear
deer	brown bear	grey wolf
mule deer	salmon	timber wolf
beaver	black bear	Russian wolfhound

Animal Rights

During the novel *The Call of the Wild*, there are many instances of animal cruelty. Brainstorm with a partner to write down as many instances of cruelty as you can from the time Buck was thrown into the railroad car to his meeting with John Thornton. (The cruelty does not need to be restricted to Buck alone.)

Now that you have your examples, choose one that, for you, represents the most flagrant example of cruelty. Then, use the rest of the page to write a letter to a newspaper editor, advocating justice and/or reform as far as this issue of abuse is concerned. Your letter should state the problem, cite examples from the book, and conclude with the action you believe citizens need to take. Your letter should be addressed to the *Dawson Star News*.

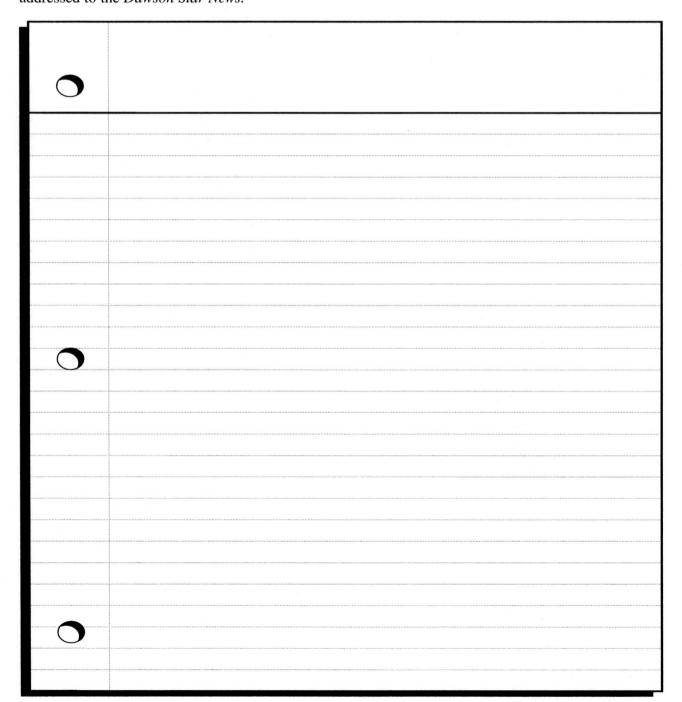

Illustrated and Captioned Time Line

There are many events that take place throughout the novel. For this activity, you will be working in small cooperative groups. What you will do is create an illustrated and captioned time line indicating some major events. This will be accomplished in three steps.

The first thing you must do is to list 10 of the major events that happen during the course of the novel. Next, you will draw 10 preliminary sketches reflecting the events. As a group, make corrections and additions to these sketches. The third step will be to draw your illustrated and captioned time line on a piece of butcher paper. To make the time line, block off 10 spaces on the butcher paper and draw your final drawings. Remember to use a felt pen to add the captions that go along with your illustrations.

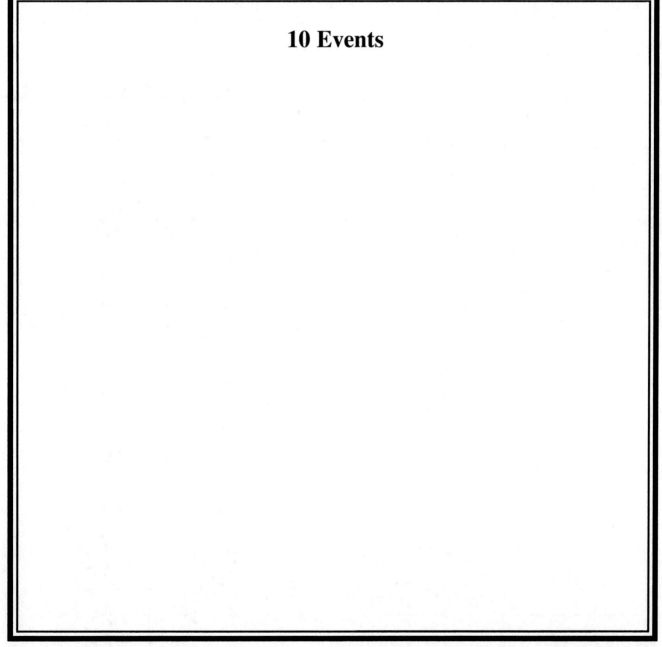

10 Events

Dramatizing a Favorite Scene

The illustrated time line that you created will no doubt serve to help you recall some of your favorite portions of the novel. Now, it is time to have fun with some of the scenes. In this next activity, you will again be working in cooperative learning groups as determined by your teacher. These groups will be larger than usual because to complete the activity will require a greater number of people.

Once you are in your group, you will need to decide which of the many scenes from the book you want to present to the class. Keep in mind what is involved in the scene and from that determine how many parts there are to be played, both the characters and the props. For instance, the river might be represented by three people lying on the floor. They can simulate the rapids by roaring and raising up on their hands and knees from time to time. The tall spruce trees by John Thornton's camp might take approximately three to five people. They can stand tall or bent and crooked and sway with the wind. However you interpret the props is your decision.

After you have picked your scene, you will have to rewrite it so that it can be dramatized. This is just what happens when a book is sold to a movie company. It has to be rewritten for film or the stage. Now, you get to see how this works. As you rewrite the scene, you will make arrangements for your rivers, trees, rocks, and so forth.

This next step is the fun part. You need to pick members from your group to play the various parts of your scene and to practice the scene. Remember to re-evaluate the scene as a group to see whether there should be any changes before you present it to the class. People who are the props (rivers, trees, etc.) are very important and should stay in character throughout the entire scene, otherwise, they will detract from the scene. When you are ready, present your scene for the class. Have fun!

Notes

_____

_____

_____

_____

_____

_____

_____

_____

_____

_____

_____

_____

_____

_____

_____

Thornton's Legacy

For this activity, you will once again enter the world of make-believe. Pretend that on the first reading of the book, the editor's nephews and nieces thought it was somehow incomplete. They were so impressed with John Thornton that they did not want him to just vanish from the earth and from the memories of his friends in Dawson. After all, they reasoned, he was the best loved of all Buck's masters and they had a special respect for one another. Also, he was respected by the other adventurers and gold seekers in Dawson. To just have him vanish with no explanation was too much to expect.

What he and Buck proposed was that a legend be created for him as to his life and what happened to him out in the wilderness while prospecting for gold. They convinced their uncle, the editor, that a short afterward be added to the novel to add such an explanation of his disappearance.

The editor has contracted you to write this legend of John Thornton and his mysterious vanishing. (This will be similar to the legend from the oldtimers about the "Lost Cabin.")

In the space provided below, write the legend of what happened to John Thornton and his dog, Buck. This tale could be related from one of the prospectors inside the old Eldorado Saloon, where their fame began. He could be telling a new arrival of the great feats of Thornton and his dog and how they went west looking for gold. Describe the scene and use details to embellish your legend.

When the class completes this activity, it will be fun to read these aloud as a culminating activity.

Objective Test and Essay

Matching: Match these quotes with the characters who said them.

1. _____ Kidnapper

2. _____ Thornton

3. _____ Mercedes

4. _____ Francois

5. _____ Hal

A. "The lazy brutes, I'll show them," he cried, preparing to lash out at them with the whip.

B. "You poor, poor dears," she cried sympathetically. "Why don't you pull hard?—then you wouldn't be whipped."

C. "God! You can all but speak!"

D. "Yep, has fits," the man said, hiding his mangled hand from the baggageman, who had been attracted by the sound of the struggle.

E. "All de tam I watch dat Buck I know for sure. Listen: some fine day him get mad an' den heem chew dat Spitz all up an' spit heem out on de snow."

True or False: Write true or false next to each statement below.

1. _____ Buck finally returns home to the warm Santa Clara Valley.

2. _____ The Yeehats and Buck become good friends after a time.

3. _____ Hal, Charles, and Mercedes are very foolish and do not belong in, nor do they respect, the wilderness.

4. _____ Buck becomes immortalized as a legend to the Yeehats.

5. _____ The forest and the call of the wild are very strong voices which call Buck back to an earlier, primeval time.

Short Answer: Provide a short answer for each of the questions below.

1. What price do Hal, Charles, and Mercedes eventually pay for their ignorance? _____

_____

2. Why does Buck have to develop the primitive ways of his ancestors? _____

_____

3. Why does Buck feel proud after he kills the Yeehats? _____

_____

4. What test do the wolves give Buck before they accept him as their leader? _____

_____

5. What does the author mean when he writes that Buck sings the song of a "younger world, which is the song of the pack"?

_____

_____

Essay: Answer these essay questions in detail on the back of this paper. Use additional paper if necessary.

1. Would John Thornton have eventually let Buck live out his life in the wilderness?

2. Just what does the author mean by the call of the wild? What is this call?

Response

Explain the meaning of each of these quotations from *The Call of the Wild*.

Chapter 1: "Buck did not read the newspapers, or he would have known that trouble was brewing, not alone for himself, but for every tidewater dog, strong of muscle and with warm, long hair, from Puget Sound to San Diego."

". . . no one saw them arrive at the little flag station known as College Park. This man talked with Manuel, and money chinked between them."

Chapter 2: "No lazy, sunkissed life was this, with nothing to do but loaf and be bored. Here was neither peace, nor rest, nor a moment's safety. All was confusion and action, and every moment life and limb were in peril."

"No fair play. Once down, that was the end of you. Well, he would see to it that he never went down. Spitz ran out his tongue and laughed again, and from that moment Buck hated him with a bitter and deathless hatred."

Chapter 3: "The dominant primordial beast was strong in Buck, and under the fierce conditions of trail life it grew and grew. Yet it was a secret growth. His newborn cunning gave him poise and control."

"The dark circle became a dot on the moon-flooded snow as Spitz disappeared from view. Buck stood and looked on, the successful champion, the dominant primordial beast who had made his kill and found it good."

Chapter 4: "The general tone of the team picked up immediately. It recovered its old-time solidarity, and once more the dogs leaped as one dog in the traces."

"A revolver shot rang out. The man came back hurriedly. The whips snapped, the bells tinkled merrily, the sleds churned along the trail; but Buck knew, and every dog knew, what had taken place behind the belt of river trees."

Chapter 5: " 'They told us up above that the bottom was dropping out of the trail and that the best thing for us to do was to lay over,' Hal said in response to Thornton's warning to take no more chances on rotten ice. 'They told us we couldn't make White River, and here we are.' This last with a sneering ring of triumph in it."

" . . . the sled was a quarter of a mile away. . . . Suddenly, they saw its back end drop down, as into a rut, and the gee pole, with Hal clinging to it, jerk into the air. Mercedes' scream came to their ears."

Chapter 6: "A 'miner's meeting,' called on the spot, decided that the dog had sufficient provocation, and Buck was discharged. But his reputation was made, and from that day his name spread through every camp in Alaska."

Chapter 7: "One night he sprang from sleep with a start, eager-eyed, nostrils quivering and scenting, his mane bristling in recurrent waves. From the forest came the call . . . distinct and definite as never before—a long-drawn howl, like, yet unlike, any noise made by a husky dog."

Conversations

Work in size-appropriate groups to write and perform the conversations that might have occurred in each of the following situations.

- Judge Miller and his servants discuss Buck's disappearance. *(5 people)*

- Toots and Ysabel talk about the gardener's helper, Manuel, and how they had better watch out and keep away from him. *(2 people)*

- Mollie and Alice talk with their brothers about how they miss Buck. *(4 people)*

- The man in the red sweater talks with two concerned missionaries who witnessed the ugly scene. *(3 people)*

- Curly and Buck talk on the deck of the *Narwhal* as it leaves Seattle for the north. What do they think is in store for them? *(2 people)*

- Francois and Perrault discuss what to do to prevent Spitz from killing any more valuable dogs like Curly. *(2 people)*

- Dave and Sol-leks tell Buck how to be a better sled dog and to watch out for Spitz. *(3 people)*

- Spitz and Buck talk after Spitz has just taken Buck's place in the snow. *(2 people)*

- Francois and Perrault talk about their losses after being attacked by the starving huskies. *(2 people)*

- The nine sled dogs meet after the attack by the huskies. They are discussing their futures and whether they will survive the trip. *(9 people)*

- Dolly and Sol-leks talk as Dolly tells him how she is going crazy and might "snap." *(2 people)*

- Francois and Perrault talk at night about how Buck is organizing a revolt against Spitz. *(2 people)*

- Several of the dogs discuss the manner and ferocity that Buck shows when he attacks Spitz for the last time. *(5 people)*

- Francois and Perrault brag with several men in Skagway about their record run from Dawson to Skagway. *(6 people)*

- The Scotch half-breed and Francois and Perrault discuss the qualities of the sled team that the half-breed is going to buy. *(3 people)*

- The half-breed tells Hal and Charles that the dogs need rest, and the new owners arrogantly reply that they know how to handle dogs. *(3 people)*

- A group of prospectors discuss the chances of Hal, Charles, and Mercedes ever reaching Dawson alive. *(4 people)*

- Buck and a group of dogs discuss their sorry fate in being sold to the misfits, Hal, Charles, and Mercedes. *(3 people)*

- Mercedes, Hal, and Charles are told by some old timers not to continue. They are told to hold up because the ice is rotten. *(5 people)*

- Mercedes, Hal, and Charles talk as the ice starts to break up around them and the river starts to drag them down. *(3 people)*

Bibliography of Related Reading

Fiction

Adventure Stories:

Aiken, Joan. *The Wolves of Willoughby.* Dell, 1987.

Branscum, Robbie. *The Murder of Hound Dog Bates.* Viking, 1982.

Brookins, Dana. *Alone in Wolf Hollow.* Houghton, 1978.

Budbill, David. *Snowshoe Trek to Otter River.* Bantam, 1976.

Engh, M.J. *The House in the Snow.* Watts, 1987.

George, Jean Craighead. *Julie of the Wolves.* Harper, 1972.

Houston, James. *Frozen Fire.* Macmillan, 1977.

Hyde, Dayton, O. *Island of the Loons.* Macmillan, 1984.

Moeri, Louise. *Journey to the Treasure.* Scholastic, 1986.

Morey, Walt. *Canyon Winter.* Dutton, 1972, .

O'Dell, Scott. *Island of the Blue Dolphins.* Houghton, 1960.

Pendergraft, Patricia. *Brush Mountain.* Putnam, 1989, .

Renner, Beverly Hollett. *The Hideaway Summer.* Harper, 1978.

Thomas, Jane Resh. *Courage at Indian Deep.* Houghton, 1984.

York, Carol Beach. *Takers and Returners: A Novel of Suspense.* Lodestar, 1982.

Animal Stories:

Adler, Carole S. *The Cat That Was Left Behind.* Houghton, 1981.

Anderson, LaVere. *Balto, Sled Dog of Alaska.* Gerrard, 1976.

Bagnold, Enid. *National Velvet.* Morrow, 1985.

Balch, Glenn. *Buck, Wild.* Harper, 1976.

Brown, F.K. *Last Hurdle.* Lianet, 1988.

Burnford, Sheila. *The Incredible Journey.* Little, 1961.

Callen, Larry. *Pinch.* Little, 1976.

DeJong, Meindert. *Along Came a Dog.* Harper, 1958,.

Denzel, Justin F. *Showfoot: White Reindeer of the Arctic.* Gerrard, 1988.

Gauch, Patricia L. *Kate, Alone.* Putnam, 1980.

Gibson, Fred. *Old Yeller.* Harper, 1956.

Hallstead, William F. *Tundra.* Crown, 1984.

Kjelgaard, James. *Big Red.* Holiday, 1945.

London, Jack. *White Fang.* Airmont, 1985.

Morey, Walt. *Scrub Dog of Alaska.* Dalton, 1971.

North, Sterling. *The Wolfling.* Scholastic, 1980.

Rawls, Wilson. *Where the Red Fern Grows.* Bantam, 1974.

Shura, Mary Francis. *Mister Wolf and Me.* Scholastic, 1982.

Taylor, Theodore. *The Trouble With Tuck.* Doubleday, 1981.

Nonfiction:

Brickenden, Jack. *Canada.* Brookwright, 1989.

Brickenden, Jack. *We Live in Canada.* Watts, 1985.

Lambie, Beatrice R. *The Mackenzie: River to the Top of the World.* Gerrard, 1967.

Answer Key

Page 10

1. Accept appropriate responses.
2. Buck has a very pleasant life at the judge's house.
3. Buck is part shepherd and St. Bernard.
4. Manuel is involved with the Chinese lottery where he gambles.
5. Buck goes willingly with Manuel because Buck trusts humans.
6. He lies because he does not want to admit that the dog attacked him since he was not the owner.
7. The train takes Buck up north to Seattle.
8. He trains Buck to fear the club and hatchet by beating him.
9. He learns not to attack a man with a club.
10. The snow is new to Buck, and he jumps around in it and is ashamed because the men laugh at him.

Page 15

1. Accept appropriate responses.
2. Curly was knocked off his feet and killed by the dogs.
3. He learns never to get knocked off his feet in a fight.
4. They were all buried in the snow.
5. He was a mail courier and had to travel swiftly.
6. Francois did this so Buck could learn from them.
7. He meant that Buck was learning his job quickly.
8. If he did not eat quickly, the others would steal his food.
9. He hated Spitz because Spitz laughed when Curly was killed.
10. He began to steal food and let others take the blame.

Page 19

1. He meant that the dogs were not civilized.

2-4. Accept appropriate answers.

Page 20

1. Accept appropriate responses.
2. He wanted to fight this dog.
3. The first fight took place after Spitz took Buck's sleeping place.
4. The fight stopped due to the whole camp being attacked by starving huskies.
5. Thirty Mile River was considered difficult due to the rapids not freezing. This forced sleds to travel the edges of the ice, which was difficult.
6. Perrault's technique was to walk in front of the sled with a long pole which he would thrust beneath the snow to see whether it would support their weight. It was slow because sometimes he fell through the ice crust and had to be dried out.
7. The driver made little leather boots for Buck's feet.
8. Dolly let out a blood-curdling howl.
9. The lack of discipline caused the dogs to fight among themselves instead of working as a team.
10. Buck broke each foreleg of Spitz during their fight.

Answer Key *(cont.)*

Page 22
1. Northwest
2. British
3. Alaska
4. Beaufort Sea
5. Yukon
6. plateau
7. Saint Elias
8. Logan
9. Canada
10. Mackenzie
11. Selwyn
12. Salmon
13. Klondike
14. Dawson
15. Whitehorse

Page 25
1. Accept appropriate responses.
2. The trip took longer due to the dogs' tiredness.
3. They were a bedraggled group.
4. They only had five days of rest.
5. He knew that they had poor knowledge of the North and were a slipshod operation.
6. They only had four days of rest.
7. They packed it with heavy things on the top which resulted in it overturning on the first turn.
8. The citizens told them to cut half the weight and use twice the dogs.
9. They were not impressed with the new dogs and had a bleak outlook of their future.
10. It means that the ice collapsed into the river.

Page 30
1. Accept appropriate responses.
2. He loves Thornton because Thornton loves his dogs like children.
3. He teaches him to never abuse his master.
4. Accept appropriate responses as to how Buck got banged around in the current on the rocks.
5. They threw their gear in the air when Buck moved the sled.
6. They were going to search for the Lost Cabin gold mine.
7. The mine was situated underneath the cabin. They would be rich.
8. The camp was being wiped out by Indians.
9. He was proud because he had killed the noblest animal of all.
10. They call him that because he is everywhere at once, causing death to the unwary.

Answer Key *(cont.)*

Page 32

1.	$1,200	6.	$1,800
2.	$60,000	7.	$90,000
3.	$3,000,000	8.	$4,500,000
4.	$4,500,000	9.	$6,750,000
5.	$1,500,000	10.	$2,250,000

Page 42

Matching

1. D
2. C
3. B
4. E
5. A

True or False

1. False
2. False
3. True
4. True
5. True

Short Answer

1. They die.
2. He must develop their ways to survive.
3. He had killed the noblest game of all.
4. They attack him from all sides, and he beats them back.
5. Buck reverts to a primitive, simpler time.

Essay

1. Accept appropriate responses. The answers should reflect a consistency in Thornton's personality. The reasons should substantiate a clear line of thinking.
2. Accept appropriate responses. The students should catch the idea that nature is wild and primitive in its natural state. In that state, all who enter it will return to their origins, which in this case are wild.

Page 43

Accept all reasonable and well supported answers.

Page 44

Perform the conversations in class. Ask students to respond to the conversations in several ways, such as, "Are the words the characters say in keeping with their personalities as developed by the author?" or "If the dogs could have talked, would they have initiated that conversation?"

48